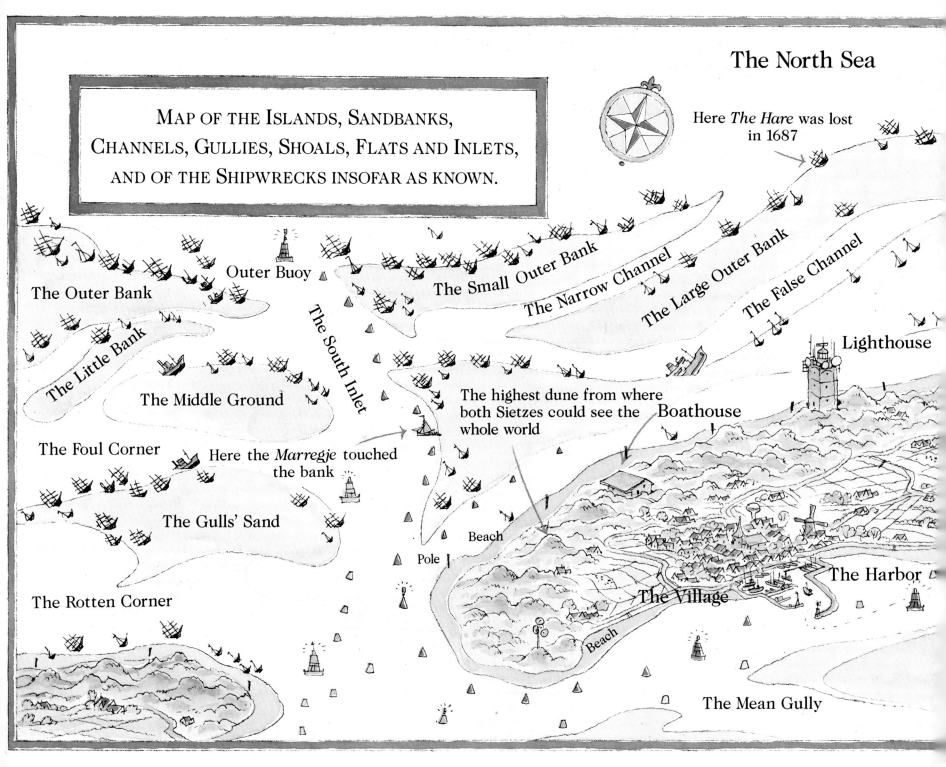

The North Sea

MAP OF THE ISLANDS, SANDBANKS,
CHANNELS, GULLIES, SHOALS, FLATS AND INLETS,
AND OF THE SHIPWRECKS INSOFAR AS KNOWN.

Here *The Hare* was lost
in 1687

Outer Buoy

The Outer Bank

The Small Outer Bank

The Narrow Channel

The Large Outer Bank

The False Channel

The Little Bank

The South Inlet

Lighthouse

The Middle Ground

The highest dune from where
both Sietzes could see the
whole world

Boathouse

The Foul Corner

Here the *Marregje* touched
the bank

The Gulls' Sand

Beach

Pole

The Rotten Corner

The Village

The Harbor

Beach

The Mean Gully

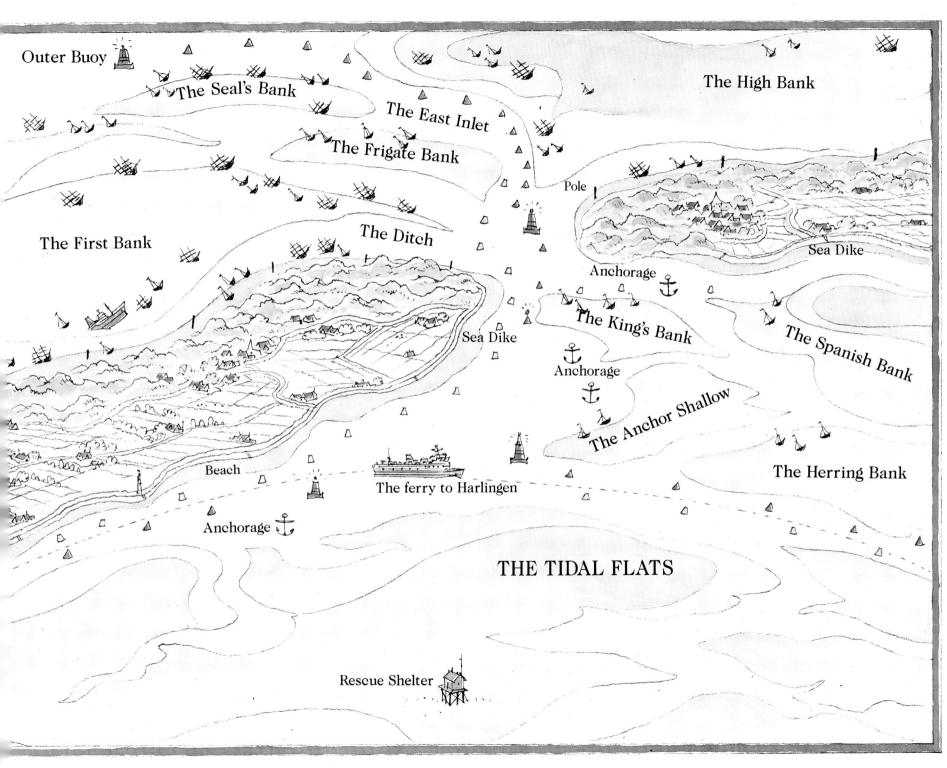

Outer Buoy

The Seal's Bank

The East Inlet

The High Bank

The Frigate Bank

Pole

The First Bank

The Ditch

Sea Dike

Anchorage

The King's Bank

Sea Dike

The Spanish Bank

Anchorage

The Anchor Shallow

Beach

The ferry to Harlingen

The Herring Bank

Anchorage

THE TIDAL FLATS

Rescue Shelter

Father, May I Come?
Written and illustrated by Peter Spier
A Doubleday Book for Young Readers

One day in the winter of 1687 Sietze Hemmes walked home through the dunes of a North Sea island off the Dutch coast. As usual he clambered up the highest dune, but today he was almost blown down by the howling wind. From up there you could see the whole world: the tiled roofs of the village, the church, the meadows, the great sea dike, and the endless deserted tidal flats. On a clear day you could also see the neighboring islands and the Frisian mainland, but not on a day like this. When Sietze turned around he saw the large breakers rolling almost to the foot of the dunes and through the spray the wild surf far away on the outer banks. There was nothing else to be seen. It was then that he saw the ship being driven helplessly onto the outer banks. Quickly he slid down the dune and ran home as fast as he could crying, "Ship on the banks! A ship in trouble!" He was out of breath when he entered his father's inn shouting, "Father, a ship on the outer banks!" Hemmo Hemmes, keeper of The Spouting Whale, as well as skipper of the lifeboat, yanked off his apron, threw it on the counter, and said, "Quick, boy, go tell the others!"

He called to his wife in the back, "Mother, there's a ship on the banks!" then grabbed his hat and coat, and hurried out the front door to the boat in its house in the dunes.

Sietze ran through the village,
raising his father's crew.

The first was Kees Schol,
blacksmith, first oar,

then Jan Visser,
caretaker of the church, second oar.

After him Doeke Cupido,
carpenter, third oar,

Douwe Lieuwen, grocer, fourth oar,

and…his brother Jaep, clogmaker, fifth oar.

And just outside the village, the last one, Tjeerd Smit, farmer, sixth oar.

The heavy boat on an even heavier wagon was pushed outside by her crew. Nearby farmers, who had rushed there with their horses, hooked them to the wagon and hauled it rocking and swaying to the beach. The crew was already on board when Sietze called out over the roar of the sea, "Father, may I come?"

But his father called back, "No, not until you're bigger."

The long oars were placed in their locks. Skipper Hemmes steadied himself and his heavy steering oar against the boat and gave the signal. The boat was then launched into the foaming surf by the yelling farmers and their ten nervously snorting horses.

The boat was lifted skyward till she stood almost on end and disappeared behind a huge breaking wave. It took all the crew's strength to get her up the next one, and slowly she made her way through wave after wave to the doomed ship.

Sietze climbed a high dune to watch it all.

The crew made their way with great skill and determination to the battered herring buss, which had already lost most of her masts and rigging and was now being buried time and again under towering ground swells. It took the crew almost four hours, but they succeeded in rescuing the five men on board the ship. And their dog.

The crew of *The Hare,* out of Enkhuizen, was taken in and well cared for by the compassionate islanders. That Sunday the minister praised the Lord for His hand in the successful rescue, and for His great goodness, given the many barrels of herring that were washed up on the beach. He even remembered to thank Sietze for his part in the saving of five fellowmen. But the dog was never mentioned.

More than three hundred years later another Sietze Hemmes was walking through the dunes. It was a perfect summer day, even though a stiff wind blew out of the east. As usual Sietze climbed the highest dune, because from up there you could still see the whole world. The beach was packed with tourists, and close to the shore were some windsurfers and fishermen in small boats. On the deserted tidal flats, besides the ferry on its way to the mainland and a few yachts, there was nothing unusual to be seen.

Sietze was about to go home when he saw something out of the corner of his eye: first one flare out of the south inlet, then another one. They were fired by a vessel being pulled out to sea by the wind and the outgoing tide. He ran home as fast as his legs would carry him, calling out as soon as he was in the village, "Flares! Flares in the south inlet." When he entered his father's hotel, he was out of breath and could only gasp, "Father, flares in the south inlet."

Hemmo Hemmes, skipper of the lifeboat, had only to push a button below his cash register to alert his crew through their beepers. He called, "Mother, flares in the south inlet!" before hurrying to the boathouse in the dunes, with Sietze hard on his heels.

Kees Schol, garage owner, engineer;

Jan Visser,
caretaker of the church, helmsman;

Doeke Cupido, contractor, crew member;

Douwe Lieuwen,
owner of the supermarket, radarman;

and his brother Jaep,
shoe-store owner, radio operator;

and Tjeerd Smit, farmer, driver of the tractor—were all there within ten minutes.

Since they practiced regularly, things went very smoothly. The doors to the boathouse were opened wide, and Tjeerd had the boat outside and on its way to the beach quickly.

"Who sounded the alarm?" asked the crew.

"My Sietze!" answered the proud skipper.

The crew was already on board when Sietze asked, "Father, may I come?"

The father looked down at his son for a second, then grabbed him under the arms and lifted him high so that Doeke and Kees could haul him into the boat. Then he climbed in himself.

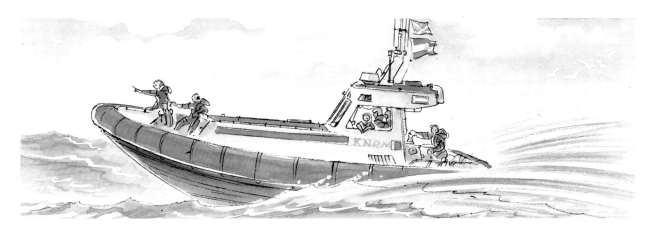

At thirty-three knots, they were alongside the sailing barge within eight minutes, just as she touched the first bank.

And who do you think were on board? Sixty-four children from Harlingen on a school trip. They were not afraid at all and were even singing!

Besides the children, there were the school's principal, three teachers, two parents, the skipper of the barge, his deckhand, their fat dog, the ship's cat, and her nine new kittens!

A tugboat salvaged the *Marregje* from Harlingen a bit later with no damage other than a stuck rudder and a ship-to-shore telephone that was on the blink.

Sietze was the hero of the day. That evening his picture and the whole story were in the

newspaper and on the late-night television news. But by then Sietze had been asleep in bed for quite a while.

That year the lifeboat was called out twenty-one more times and rescued fifty-seven adults, nine children, five dogs, eleven cats, two gerbils, and, believe it or not, one angry wet parrot!

This rigid, inflatable self-righting lifeboat, divided in four watertight compartments, is accessible through watertight hatches.

She has a half-enclosed wheelhouse with seats for four crew members, who communicate through a helmet intercom system.

The boat is designed to withstand a free-fall of 20 feet. She is self-righting up to 140°, thanks to the air chambers in the wheelhouse roof. Should the boat capsize beyond 140°, the air bag in the roof inflates automatically and will right the boat within seconds.

Length overall: 34'10"; Beam: 13'5"; Draft: 2½'; Tube diameter: 2'2"; Empty weight: 7.30 tons; Engines: 2 380HP Volvo Penta TAMD 71A; Propulsion: 2 Hamilton 291 jets; Speed: 33 knots.

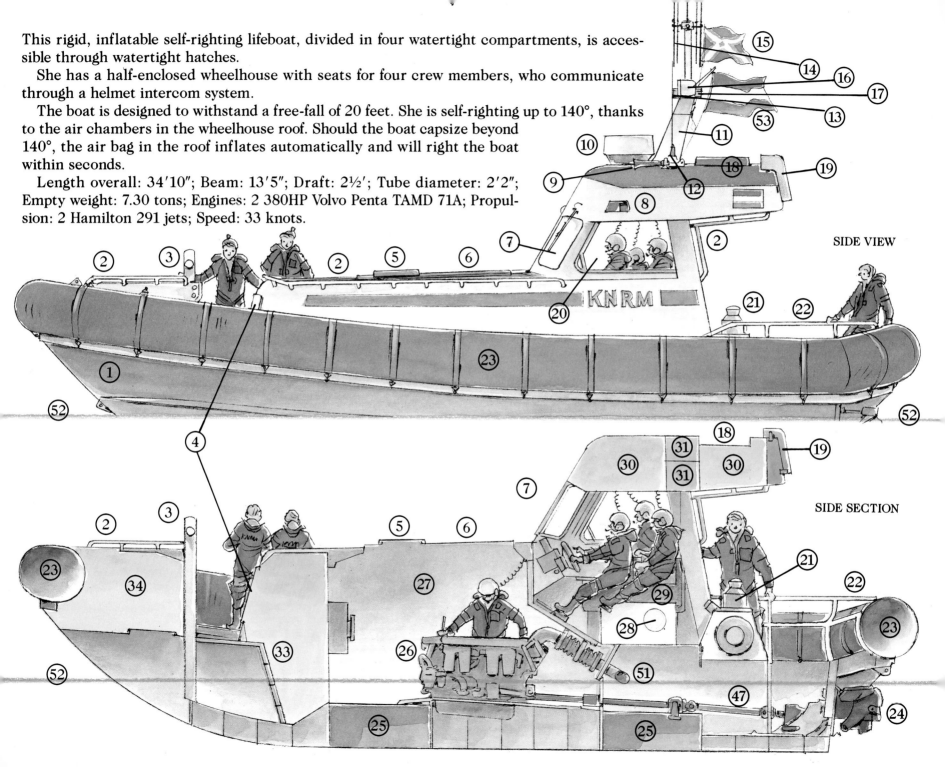

SIDE VIEW

SIDE SECTION

TOP VIEW

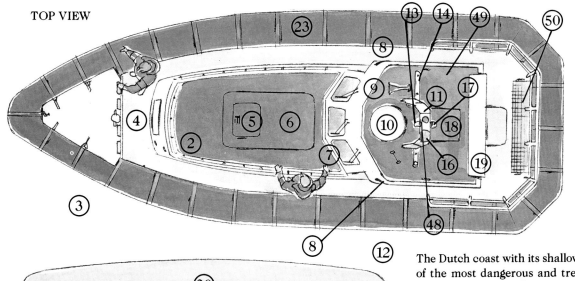

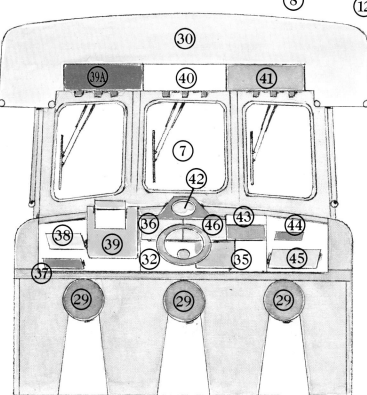

**SECTION THROUGH WHEELHOUSE
LOOKING FORWARD**

The Dutch coast with its shallow waters and shifting sandbanks and channels has always been one of the most dangerous and treacherous in the world. Sudden gales and ferocious storms have claimed thousands of vessels and countless lives during the past two thousand years.

But the people living along the coast, many of whom earned a living on the sea themselves, were always willing to risk their lives to save others. They plucked survivors from hollowed-out tree trunks, snatched them off primitive boats covered with animal hides, off Roman triremes and medieval carracks, and off galleons of the Spanish Armada, which came to grief there in 1588....

A bit of beachcombing on the side was always welcome. One nineteenth-century sermon even implored "...and if it is Thy will that a ship be lost today, Heavenly Father, please let it be here!"

Saving lives had always been a private enterprise until the Royal Netherlands Rescue Society (Koninklijke Nederlandse Redding Maatschappij) was established in 1824, a few months after the founding of the British Royal Lifeboat Institution. Most other European nations followed their example, and today more than thirty-five maritime rescue organizations exist around the globe.

Virtually all the crews of the Dutch lifeboats—manning more than fifty vessels of twelve different types—are volunteers, as are the local commissions. The Society is funded solely through voluntary contributions.

Since 1824 the KNRM has saved more than thirty thousand lives.

When collecting the material for this book, I sailed aboard the newest lifeboat stationed on one of the islands in the North Sea.

The skipper was the only crew member on the Society's payroll. The others were volunteers: the island's barber, the village mailman, a housepainter, a bricklayer, a mechanic....

Today's alarms are not sounded for East Indiamen, galleons, or fishing schooners but for supertankers, container ships, giant floating drydocks, pleasure craft, surfers, and missing aircraft.

No matter how monstrous the storm, no matter how dangerous the situation, night or day, summer or winter, the lifeboats answer the call without fail—as they always have!

And what do today's rescuers think of their work? "We don't think, because if we started thinking, we'd stay home! Thinking...? You fly out the door when the alarm is sounded...you race to the boat...*you sail!*"

So you see that nothing has really changed, not counting the boats and the electronics. The men of today think exactly as their ancestors did for twenty centuries!

Other books by Peter Spier:

THE FOX WENT OUT ON A CHILLY NIGHT
PETER SPIER'S MOTHER GOOSE LIBRARY
    LONDON BRIDGE IS FALLING DOWN!
    TO MARKET! TO MARKET!
    HURRAH, WE'RE OUTWARD BOUND!
    AND SO MY GARDEN GROWS
OF DIKES AND WINDMILLS
THE ERIE CANAL
GOBBLE, GROWL, GRUNT
CRASH! BANG! BOOM!
FAST-SLOW, HIGH-LOW
THE STAR-SPANGLED BANNER
TIN-LIZZIE
NOAH'S ARK
OH, WERE THEY EVER HAPPY!
BORED—NOTHING TO DO!
THE LEGEND OF NEW AMSTERDAM
PEOPLE
PETER SPIER'S VILLAGE BOOKS
    BILL'S SERVICE STATION
    FIREHOUSE
    THE TOY SHOP
    THE PET STORE
    FOOD MARKET
    MY SCHOOL
PETER SPIER'S RAIN
PETER SPIER'S CHRISTMAS!
PETER SPIER'S LITTLE BIBLE STORYBOOKS
    THE CREATION
    NOAH
    JONAH
PETER SPIER'S LITTLE ANIMAL BOOKS
    LITTLE CATS
    LITTLE DOGS
    LITTLE DUCKS
    LITTLE RABBITS
THE BOOK OF JONAH
DREAMS
WE THE PEOPLE
PETER SPIER'S CIRCUS!